From Ordinary
TO *Extraordinary*

by Diana Torruella Gaines

"Why not?"

The answer to my "Why not?" was
*"Why not reinvent myself as a real estate developer
and start with my own city of Baltimore?"*

This is the story of how the 200 block of North Madeira Street
was transformed by a rookie developer
using Baltimore City's award-winning
Vacants to Value Program.

How do you complete your "Why not" question?

From Ordinary ^{TO} *Extraordinary*

First Printing

Cover design and book layout by
Janice "Jago" Goulart
jago_artdesign@yahoo.com

ISBN: 978-1-499661-72-9

Printed in the United States of America

*To Steve,
who gave me the unconditional love
and support to be "me."*

"Steve and I were renting an apartment in Bolton Hill prior to moving onto Madeira Street. We were getting married (last September) and knew we wanted a house to start our lives together in. We looked for over a year, and nothing really "fit." After we got married, we went out to look at a few more houses and Madeira Street was on our list to see. As soon as we saw it, we knew that was where we wanted to live. We loved that the house was recently rehabbed, but that the neighborhood was still considered "up and coming," and we were very excited at the investment opportunity we had in this house. We were able to use the $10,000 Vacant to Value Booster grant incentive to assist us with our purchase. We are thrilled with our decision and can't imaging living anywhere else. We have a great group of neighbors, and watching the area grow and move forward is extremely rewarding and continues to validate our decision to purchase."
—Andrea & Steve

Madeira Residents

Contents

Acknowledgements

I would like to thank the individuals that made
my journey on Madeira complete.

To Kevin Butler, my general contractor: Thank you for being patient, trustworthy and disciplined. Your commitment to the project was as strong as mine! Thank you for building a product that I could sell and making the process fun. Finally, thank you for your friendship.

To the wonderful staff at Baltimore Housing: You know who you are! Thank you for guiding me through the Vacants to Value Program and the development process in the city. Your help and support were invaluable!

To Mayor Stephanie Rawlings-Blake: Thank you for being a visionary, and creating and supporting a program that allowed me to reinvent myself. May Vacants to Value continue to grow and develop so you can meet your goal of welcoming 10,000 new families to Baltimore.

To the New Baltimoreans that have purchased a home on the 200 Block of North Madeira Street: Ryan, Andrea and Steve, Jason, Daria, Marjorie, Matt, James and Amanda, and Stephanie: Thank you for making the Tu Casa houses your homes and for believing in the vitality of the project. You are a true gift to Baltimore City!

To Janice "Jago" Goulart, my irreplaceable Sr. Graphic Designer: Thank you for helping me transform an ordinary file into an extraordinary manuscript. Your patience and talent are endless!

And to Steve, Charlie, Corey and Bennett: You know how much I love you! Thanks for supporting my vision and your countless visits to Madeira. You are amazing!

Prologue

The redevelopment of the 200 block of North Madeira Street was the result of the answer to a simple question: "Why not...?" I did not have a traditional "aha" moment. Instead, I had a "Why not" moment.

In September of 2010, I was a homemaker looking for a venture to complement my stay at home status. I wanted to be able to capitalize on the strengths that my background provided: a fully bilingual upbringing with a complete understanding of two very different cultures, a solid education from Duke University, many years as a banker specializing in Health Care Lending, and a firm commitment to community service. Simply stated, I wanted to be able to make money and make a difference.

I evaluated many options over the course of several months. Baltimore Mayor Stephanie Rawlings-Blake's award winning and nationally recognized Vacants to Value Program (V2V) was the answer to my search. Three main components sealed my decision. First, V2V provided a simple path that I could follow; the application process was straightforward and the staff managing it exceptional. Second, a $10,000 Booster Incentive available for down payment and closing costs was a very valuable asset to potential V2V home buyers. Finally, investing in a city was consistent with my belief that our country's economic resurgence would begin in our inner cities, *so why not start with my own city of Baltimore?*

It is significant to note that this manuscript contains two stories, both essential components of the achievements on Madeira. First, it documents the chain of events that resulted in the physical redevelopment of the 200 block of North Madeira Street in Baltimore City from "Ordinary to Extraordinary", or as Mayor Rawlings-Blake would say, "Vacants to Value". The second is a story of friendship, namely the development of a very improbable one. It was the search for a general contractor that led to Mr. Kevin Butler. The manuscript documents how a northern Baltimore County mom and an inner city contractor found a common passion that served as the foundation for a solid redevelopment effort and what promises to be a life-long friendship.

The answer to my Why not was "Why not reinvent myself as a real estate developer and start with my own City of Baltimore?" I never anticipated that the response would turn into one of the most personally fulfilling accomplishments of my life.

How do you complete your "Why not" question?

*Side Wall that Frames the Entrance to the
200 Block of North Madeira Street, Before and After*

Part One:
"We Found"

The Journey Begins

My journey into the field of real estate development began as the passionate offspring of a desire to identify an income-producing effort that would result in an improvement in the community. That's the beauty of passion; it gives you the fuel you need to see an effort to its end. I am Hispanic, and one thing Hispanics are full of, every single on one us, is passion. I was also driven by a desire to give back to a city that had been so good to me. Over the course of the previous 30 years, I had met my husband of 25 years, raised three sons, nurtured lifetime friendships, and had established myself financially in Baltimore.

The journey is full of what I consider to be acceptable financial accomplishments and immeasurable personal enrichment. Over the course of approximately 3 years, an entire city block was transformed from an area characterized by blight, abandonment and drugs, to a completely redeveloped community street. I also met some remarkable individuals, the most important being my general contractor, Mr. Kevin Butler. My business relationship with Kevin provided the solid foundation that my vision required from a craft standpoint. But more importantly, the personal relationship that we would develop over time would create a very special connection based on respect, and above all, trust. This relationship would prove to be invaluable when the project got difficult.

My experience developing row homes in Baltimore City was far from uneventful. During the course of the three years developing on the 200 block of North Madeira Street, I would feel like the target of carefully organized schemes, face a workman's compensation lawsuit, and lose thousands of dollars in the form of stolen construction materials. Despite all the moral and material challenges, I remained focused on the redevelopment efforts.

The selection process of where to develop was a tedious one. I knew that I wanted to be in east Baltimore and capitalize on the dynamics generated by the world-renown Johns Hopkins Hospital. Many sites located in this footprint were evaluated for potential development, most often resulting in the same answer: "It is part of EBDI". Approximately 13 years ago, East Baltimore Development, Inc. (EBDI), was established by a consortium of community, government, institutional and charitable entities to revive and restart the east Baltimore neighborhood located in John Hopkins Hospital's footprint. My challenge was to identify a group of homes that did not belong to EBDI.

3

In September of 2011, I finally settled on a cluster of six row homes located on the 200 block of North Madeira Street, in the Middle East Neighborhood of east Baltimore. These 6 row homes were part of the Vacants to Value Program's portfolio of available properties. Over the course of the next few years, through painfully piecing purchases from the city, private owners and receivership auctions, I would come to own 10 out of 20 properties on the 200 block of North Madeira Street. A quiet, one way street located 4 blocks east of the Johns Hopkins Hospital main campus became my new passion, and with Mr. Kevin Butler as my contractor and my husband Steve as my banker, the redevelopment adventure began.

What follows is the story of how the 200 block of North Madeira was transformed from "Vacant to Value" or "Ordinary to Extraordinary".

Vacants to Value (V2V) Program

In November of 2010, Baltimore City Mayor Stephanie Rawlings-Blake and Baltimore Housing Commissioner Paul Graziano announced a combined effort to reduce vacant housing and blight in Baltimore. Like many other inner cities across the nation, Baltimore had watched its population decline steadily over the past decade. The city had become home to over 16,000 vacant structures, with almost 4,000 being city-owned. The Mayor announced a goal of welcoming 10,000 new families to Baltimore City by 2020, and the new Vacants to Value Program was going to precipitate home ownership. In an incredible effort that required the participation of many city agencies and included property tax cuts, infrastructure repairs, demolition, and housing, the Mayor pledged a strong commitment to ridding Baltimore of blight. In November of 2012, Mayor Rawlings-Blake committed to demolish or rehabilitate 3,000 vacant houses over 3 years under the Clinton Global Initiative, Committee to Action effort.

Baltimore City's Vacants to Value Program is based on the implementation of six specific strategies:

1) the disposition of city-owned properties
2) simplified code enforcement in stronger markets
3) the enablement of investment in emerging markets
4) the accessibility to home buyer incentives
5) the support of large scale redevelopment in distressed areas
6) targeted demolition in highly distressed blocks

Baltimore Housing maintains a list of all properties available for purchase under the V2V Program on the Program's website, **www.vacantstovalue.org**. The website also details home buyer incentives, the property acquisition process, and contains the necessary application forms.

After carefully researching the Program, I was certain I wanted to be a Vacants to Value Developer. V2V was expertly crafted to be attractive to both developers and homebuyers. The Program provided immediate inventory and homebuyer assistance.

I am very proud to say that the properties on the 200 block of North Madeira were among the first to be sold by Baltimore City under the Vacants to Value Program.

5

Recognizing that a redevelopment effort required assistance for homebuyers, the Mayor grouped home buying incentives under **B-HiP!**, the Baltimore Homeownership Incentive Program. The incentives are specifically tailored for Baltimore City homebuyers. The most impressive and attractive aspect of these incentives is that they are stackable, meaning that one individual can receive more than one incentive. Several of the buyers on Madeira came to closing with over $18,000 in incentives.

All incentive programs require the completion of a homeownership counseling process at a city approved agency, $1,000 in homebuyer personal funds towards the purchase of a property, an appraisal, and a home inspection. The homeownership counseling process has two steps, completion of a course and participation in a one on one counseling session. The entire process must be completed in its entirety prior to executing a contract to purchase a home. Baltimore City homebuyers should secure the Home Counseling Certificate prior to beginning the home search to prevent delays in the ability to submit a contract. The Home Counseling Program provided by the Southeast Community Development Corporation was particularly efficient. Potential homebuyers could complete the class requirement of the certificate online, at **www.southeastcdc.org**, and schedule the required one on one counseling session thereafter.

Only homes that have been subject to a Vacant Building Notice for 12 months or more prior to their rehabilitation are eligible for the Vacants to Value Booster Program, the $10,000 V2V homebuyer incentive. Every home redeveloped by Tu Casa on the 200 block of North Madeira Street had received a Vacant Building Notice. Thus, all Tu Casa homebuyers were eligible for and received the V2V $10,000 Booster Incentive.

V2V has proven to be a very effective program in Baltimore City and the new homeowners on the 200 Block of North Madeira Street are a testament to its success.

Mandy Breedlove, Baltimore Housing
Assistance Director, Land Transactions
Interior of 212 North Madeira
First Unit Redeveloped

Historic Restoration and Rehabilitation Tax Credit (CHAP)

The Historic Restoration and Rehabilitation Tax Credit certified by the Commission for Historical and Architectural Preservation (CHAP) is Baltimore City's first tax credit intended to benefit the owners of historically designated properties. This 10 year tax credit freezes real estate property tax assessments at pre-rehabilitation costs. Under the V2V Program, this meant freezing real estate taxes at the costs of the shell to the developer.

Baltimore City CHAP Property Tax Credit
Cost Savings Comparison
218 North Madeira: assume a new $160,000 assessment
upon sale of the property

	218 N. Madeira with CHAP	218 N. Madeira without CHAP	
Assessed Value Based on Developer Cost of Shell	$10,000	$160,000	Assessment Upon Sale of Property
City Property Tax Rate	2.260%	2.260%	City Property Tax Rate
City Property Taxes	$226.00	$3,616.00	City Property Taxes
State Tax Rate (.12%)	$192.00	$192.00	State Tax Rate (.12%)
Annual Property Taxes	$418.00	$3,808.00	Annual Property Taxes
Monthly Property Taxes	$35.00	$317.00	Monthly Property Taxes
Total Taxes Paid Over a 10 Year Period	$4,200.00	$38,040.00	Total Taxes Paid Over a 10 Year Period
Cost Savings to Buyer Over a 10 Year Period	$33,840.00		

Prepared by Neil Junker, O'Connell & Associates, Historic Tax Credit Consultants, Baltimore, MD

The row homes located on Madeira were part of the East Monument Historic District, and thus qualified for CHAP consideration. There are two steps to obtaining CHAP certification. First, you must file an application prior to starting any construction; failure to do so will compromise your ability to obtain the credits. Once a preliminary approval letter is issued, you may start construction. A final certification request is filed when construction is completed, a Use and Occupancy Permit is in hand, and your contractor has been paid in full. Allow approximately 30 days for the processing of the final certification letter to be issued by CHAP.

As a developer, securing CHAP for a unit would save the potential homebuyer tens of thousands of dollars in real estate taxes. Additionally, the lower monthly property taxes made the row home affordable to individuals with a wider financial profile.

The good news is that many Tu Casa properties were approved for CHAP. The bad news is that I was not aware of this incredible advantage until I had already fully redeveloped 4 homes.

Property Acquisition

There are basically five ways to purchase city properties: private sales, bank foreclosures, tax sales, through the Vacants to Value Program, and receivership. In addition to V2V property purchases, receivership properties proved to be helpful to the redevelopment efforts on Madeira, albeit for a very limited period of time.

Baltimore City's Receivership Program, described in Section 121 of the city's Building, Fire and Related Codes, was established to reclaim vacant properties. In order to take a property into receivership, the city must identify a Partner in Receivership. This partner agrees to bid on the property at a public auction but is not guaranteed to be the purchaser because the law requires that the receivership property be sold to the highest bidder.

I agreed to be the city's Partner in Receivership for all eligible units on the 200 block of North Madeira Street. Vacant property owners of record started facing the city in court, and any structures that were not rehabilitated were auctioned by One House at a Time, Inc. (OHAAT), the city's Vacant Building Receiver. I purchased three properties from OHAAT at receivership auctions in 2012 and through early 2013. However, by mid-2013, development efforts and sales on Madeira had attracted speculative investors. The prices for the remaining receivership properties on the block escalated to ridiculous levels. Simply stated:

Property acquisition costs + Rehabilitation costs > Market sales price

I could not afford to pay inflated prices for shells that were to be completely gutted. Visions of rehabilitating the block for homeownership were significantly truncated.

Unfortunately for Tu Casa, receivership efforts on the 200 block of North Madeira Street had metamorphosed into the worst possible outcome: a pool for speculative activity.

Branding: Tu Casa Development Group

I knew what I wanted to do, redevelop houses for homeownership using the V2V Program, and where, in Baltimore City. Now I had to figure out how.

The most powerful feature about branding a new product is that you, the creator, control most of the variables. I wanted to be known for consistency and credibility. I was going to differentiate my row homes by building a reasonably priced product whose basic amenities greatly exceeded the current inventory on the market. I knew I wanted to offer buyers completely finished basements, higher ceilings, luxurious interior finishes, wood decks and parking options. I also wanted the exterior of the homes to be unique and incorporate features such as dual entrance lighting and brick flower boxes.

After much thought, I named the company Tu Casa Development Group and set the legal entity up as a Limited Liability Corporation, (LLC). An LLC structure limited personal liability to the amount invested in the company. I decided to call the entity Tu Casa Development Group because it was very representative of my Hispanic roots: "Tu Casa...Your Home."

The original tagline of "Turn Our House into Your Home" was just a starting point. I believe that a changing slogan is a sign of growth, experience and innovation. I was completely captivated by the process of taking something vacant and ordinary, and turning it into something occupied and extraordinary. After the first unit was completed, I coined the term "Transforming Properties from Ordinary to Extraordinary" as the new company tagline and called the cluster "Casitas at Madeira".

All marketing products were developed in-house and were ordered from a very affordable internet provider. Oversized post cards proved to be very versatile and cost effective, having front and back areas to showcase the product.

It was very beneficial to develop a comprehensive website. I discovered that many prospective buyers had taken the time to find and study the Tu Casa website, **www.tucasabaltimore.com**.

Another key differentiator of a Tu Casa property would be that, except for a 6 month period when 2 properties were listed with a realtor, I would receive every incoming call of interest.

The 200 block of North Madeira Street was going to have a very unique and exciting story and I was going to be the one to tell it.

Construction Budget

Fully committed to being a Vacants to Value Developer in the city of Baltimore, the first step in my development plan was to determine costs. How much money did I need to do this? I kept telling myself that if I could finance up to nine figure long term care facility portfolios, I could certainly manage the rehabilitation of a six figure row home.

I had spent almost a decade as a commercial lender specializing in Health Care and learning from a magnificent mentor, Mr. William N. Apollony. Bill gave me a $2.00 bill back in 1988, which I still carry in my wallet. He taught me to be driven, fearless and, like the $2.00 bill, unique. Bill used to say "Everybody's money is green. We just need to differentiate ourselves." And we did, through extensive knowledge and superior customer service. I was going to apply this same principle to the development of Madeira. My new "everybody" was other inner city developers and their inventory. Everybody's units were built with wood and drywall. However, the totality of the rehabilitation of Tu Casa's units would be a key differentiator. I would also strive to provide excellent customer service.

I can't possibly stress enough the importance of generating a realistic and comprehensive development budget. There are many different costs associated with real estate development, and they are incurred at different times. I chose to divide them into four categories: hard construction costs, soft construction costs, real estate carrying costs and selling costs. Setting a comprehensive budget also helped me identify some of the nuances of doing business in Baltimore City. It was an invaluable exercise.

Hard construction costs included the property acquisition expenses, the general contract (shell redevelopment costs), appliances and a contingency reserve. Property acquisition expenses were the costs to acquire the original structure, or shell. The general contract represents the costs of rehabilitating the shell from a bricks and mortar standpoint and all development permits. It is vital that the general contractor carry Workman's Compensation and General Liability insurances as part of the agreement. Be sure to have a reliable system in place to confirm the policies are current.

It is practical to solicit several estimates for the costs to rehabilitate the shell. However, I am a firm believer in "you get what you pay for" and

13

the lowest priced construction contract may not be the best. Recognize that appliances are often not included in the general contract and can add up to $5,000 to your project costs depending on the scope of what you chose to equip the home with. Tu Casa properties were appliance-ready without further expense to the buyer and included new, stainless steel appliances in the kitchen and a stackable washer and dryer in the laundry area.

Ground Rent may be due as part of the property acquisition process. For the most part, there are two ways in which you can hold title to a property in Baltimore City, in fee simple or subject to a ground rent. Fee simple is the most common and highest form of ownership recognized by law. In fee simple, the owners have complete ownership of the land and the improvements, subject to taxes and any debt. Ground rents, very common in Baltimore City, are a recurring cash payment to whoever holds an interest in the land located directly underneath a home. Ground rent payments generally range between $50 and $150 per year and are made annually or semi-annually. They are perpetual (everlasting) and are registered with the State Department of Assessments and Taxation. However, payment is not due on ground rents that are not recorded. Most of the properties located on Madeira were subject to ground rents, but only four were recorded.

It is highly recommended to include a general contingency reserve equal to 5-10% of the total general contract amount in case an unexpected cost is identified during construction. I have learned that when it comes to vacant buildings you really never know what kind of condition the structure is going to be in until you complete the gutting. The structural integrity of the building must be carefully monitored, and vacant properties often require new footings and significant underpinning. Footings are cement supports located under a row home's foundation. Underpinning is the process of extending the foundation to support a deeper basement. Most Baltimore row homes have basements with very low ceilings or crawl space. In order to gain living space, Tu Casa property basements are excavated to a height of 7+ feet, requiring significant underpinning.

Other additional costs that may present themselves, called change orders, can create a shortage of funds and/or erase projected sales profit very easily. A change order is a variation to the scope of work that has been agreed upon in a construction contract. In theory, any change orders to the general contract are funded under the contingency reserve. A general contract should clearly define what will be considered a change order.

Soft construction costs will include Architectural and Engineering fees, settlement charges, builder's risk insurance, general liability insurance, marketing expenses and property registration costs.

Once you assume title for a Baltimore City row home, you will have to register the property. The Baltimore City Code, Article 13, Subtitle 4-2, requires every owner of a non-owner occupied dwelling unit, "whether occupied or vacant, whether it is producing revenue or not producing revenue, whether habitable or not habitable" to file a registration statement with the Housing Commissioner. This must be done upon any transfer of the property and annually on September 1st. Failure to record the property will result in the issuance of a $500.00 fine that will not be reversed. I received such a fine and went to court to contest it. I had no idea that properties had to be recorded. The only reason my fine was waived was because the inspector that issued the citation failed to appear in court. Learn from my mistakes: record your property at the Office of Permits and Code Enforcement, located on the ground floor of the Benton Building, 417 E. Fayette, Room 100, in Baltimore. Ignorance of the law is not a defense!

Ah yes, more on the transfer of ownership. Once that vacant property transfers, you will start receiving Vacant Property Notices, or mounds of letters sent via certified mail. The first time I received such a letter, approximately 5 days after settlement of the first cluster of homes, I was very confused. I was on a quest to do something good, get rid of blight, and 5 days in to my journey I started receiving what I considered to be very unpleasant mail. Remember, I purchased 6 properties. I received 24 certified letters over the course of 7 days. The city tracks vacant properties by issuing these letters, so accept them as part of the process and use them as proof that your property qualifies for the V2V Booster Incentive.

Once the property is approximately 45 days from completion, you will start incurring real estate carrying costs such as electricity, water, alarm monitoring fees, and real estate property taxes. Electricity to the property will be connected and you will start incurring electric bills. It is possible to have to pay an additional cost to connect the utility company wires to the unit. Several times I had to pay for the installation of new posts to house Baltimore Gas and Electric Company (BGE) wires. Remember that contingency reserve I suggested?

The next carrying cost will be water. Once the water is connected you will start receiving a quarterly bill. I strongly suggest determining the ease of connecting to water early in the development process. Water can be disconnected at the meter or at the water main. Connecting back to the meter is simple. Connecting back to the water main is another story, as it will require jack-hammering through the existing black top (road) to make the connection. Please note that it may take the coordination of several departments to solve one problem, as duties at a city level are quite bifurcated, (specifically divided by scope).

You will also want to consider installing an alarm system as soon as the home is wired for electricity and anything copper becomes part of the home. I once incurred a loss of $1,500 associated with the removal of approximately $200 worth of copper wiring. There are some very affordable alarm installation and monitoring packages available to home builders. A final suggestion: build a steel cage around the outdoor HVAC unit components, as the alarm won't protect them.

Very candidly, real estate taxes can be an unnecessary, expensive inconvenience. V2V properties will generally be assessed at the price you pay for the shells. However, receivership properties will most likely be assessed at pre-vacant numbers, so it will be imperative to file a reassessment request quickly. It is not unusual to incur at least one year of taxes at the pre-vacant assessment levels due to nuances in the current policies and procedures regarding the filing of reassessments. It would be brilliant if all vacant notice properties could be instantly reassessed for property taxes at purchase price upon transfer of ownership.

A Use and Occupancy Permit is the last permit obtained as part of the construction process. Once the Use and Occupancy Permit (U&O) is issued you will have to obtain general property insurance, as the builder's risk coverage will often terminate "de facto" despite policy expiration date. A U&O establishes that the unit has passed all necessary inspections and is ready to be lived in. Any claims filed under a builder's risk policy following the issuance of a Use and Occupancy Permit could be denied. Learn from my mistakes. In my case, the theft occurred the day after the Use and Occupancy Permit had been issued.

Be mindful that once the property is ready for sale you will have to pay a Buyer Realtor fee in the range of 2.5 to 3.0% and settlement costs often up to 2.0% of property sale price. Please note that First Time Home Buyers are exempt from State Transfer Taxes in the State of Maryland, and this .25% of purchase price is paid by the seller.

In summary, a sample Comprehensive Redevelopment Budget follows.

Redevelopment Budget

Hard Costs
Property Acquisition Costs/Shell
Settlement Charges for Shell
Hard Construction Costs-Construction Contract
Contingency Reserve
Appliances

Soft Costs
Architectural and Engineering Fees
Builder's Risk Insurance
General Liability Insurance
CHAP Application Costs

Real Estate Carrying Costs
Property Registration
Ground Rent
Property Insurance
Real Estate Property Taxes
Electricity (minimum 3 months reserve recommended)
Water (2 payments)
Alarm (3 months)

Sale of Property Expenses
Marketing
Selling Costs
>   Realtor Fees
>   Seller Portion of Settlement Charges

With a comprehensive budget outlined, it was time to add hard figures to the line items and identify the source of capital.

Capital: "think.higher."

I approached over a dozen banks in the search for capital and shared my plan with one too many past colleagues to name. The answer was consistently frustrating, "We know you will succeed, but the bank is not lending for real estate construction."

One of the things I love the most about my husband is that he gives me personal and professional support to follow my dreams. Oscar Wilde once said, "Never love anyone who treats you like you're ordinary." My husband makes me feel truly extraordinary. He is a source of confidence, encouragement and love. He is my rock.

Recognizing the potential of the effort, Steve agreed to consider providing Tu Casa with the necessary funds through a combination of Gaines personal cash and an investment company called HighBank Capital Partners, (HBCP). In 2009, my husband formed a series of mid-market, investment bank and advisory firms under the name of HighBank, **www.highbank.com**. He formed the entities with the mission statement that clients deserved to have their highest expectations met. HBCP was the HighBank Companies' investment entity.

Before a penny was advanced from a personal or corporate checking account, I was going to have to prepare a Business Plan, complete with revenue, expense and profit projections. An investment in Tu Casa would have to pass the comprehensive, standard review all HBCP investments were subject to. I found myself being the epitome of a HighBank client, deserving to have my highest expectations met and given the confidence to "think.higher."

Preparing a Business Plan was tedious but necessary. It forced me to fully research the fundamentals that would impact the project. I gained a better understanding of the neighborhood's economic drivers and characteristics including average rent, median home sale, and average household income. I looked at the resident education level and unemployment rate for the neighborhood. I evaluated the competition and redevelopment efforts in the community's footprint. Analyzing all this information helped me develop a prospective buyer profile, determine a maximum (cap) on how much to spend on the development of a unit and think about a realistic asking price. My biggest challenge was going to be establishing market price. A comparable unit had not been developed or sold on Madeira in over 50 years!

Over a dozen "intense" revisions later and a minimum of 2 dozen adjustments to the numbers, the Business Plan was complete and the investment in the project was approved. Tu Casa had secured capital!

I now had a project, a company name and logo, a comprehensive Business Plan and capital. What was missing? Ah, yes...someone to build the houses.

I was in desperate need of a general contractor.

The Contractor

I called Baltimore Housing and asked for a list of contractors that had a history of building in the City without violations. With the help of the internet and a little investigative work, (driving to the neighborhoods in which these contractors were actively building), I decided to contact three individuals and asked to see a final product. A final decision was made to work with Mr. Kevin Butler, principal of Butler Management LLC.

The first time I met Kevin Butler I was very apprehensive. I was to meet him at an address by the Baltimore train station. I drove past the location about 15 minutes prior to our appointment and saw this young, African American male, heatedly talking on a cell phone. Mr. Butler was mad at someone on the other end of the telephone and perhaps this was not the best time to meet him. His bald head and arms covered in tattoos intimidated me. I almost drove away. Instead, I texted a close friend the following message: "Janet, I am meeting a contractor called Kevin Butler at (property address). His phone number is (number), just in case..." I hit Send, parked my car, and was off to meet Mr. Butler. Little did I know this would be one of the best decisions I have ever made.

Mr. Butler was nice enough. He shook my hand and was very cordial. As soon as I walked into the row home I knew I wanted to work with this man. His craftsmanship was nothing short of outstanding. The details in the construction did not go unnoticed: the rounded edges on the granite counter tops, the grooved window sills, elaborate tile work in the bathrooms, and the use of beveled glass, to name a few. This young contractor paid attention to detail, had a solid sense of combining building materials, and did not hold back on quality.

I believe that "it takes money to make money." In this particular endeavor, it meant spending money on quality materials (real hard wood floors vs. engineered wood floors, ceramic tile vs. vinyl tile) to generate returns. I wanted to find a contractor that would not sacrifice quality to make a dollar. Mr. Butler's work certainly suggested this was part of his fundamental approach to construction. The ultimate proof came in January of 2014, when Mr. Butler was finishing 229 North Madeira. He used an exquisite marble tile in the entrance. He called and said, "We now have marble on Madeira."

As we were touring the unit, Mr. Butler indicated that he was meeting me out of courtesy and had no interest in building for anyone other than himself. He informed me that he was 32 years old and had been building for approximately 5 years. He mentioned he was particularly proud of a barber shop he had developed located nearby. I asked to see the barber shop and he obliged. I quickly forgot how this man's appearance had intimidated me 30 minutes prior, and was determined to convince him to work with Tu Casa.

As we toured the barber shop, which was absolutely spectacular, I shared my vision to set a new standard in Baltimore City for what I called "affordable luxury living." I wanted to raise the bar on development and keep the prices affordable so that renters could become home buyers. My resolve seemed to surprise Mr. Butler, a lady from "the Valley" (as he called Baltimore county ladies), interested in improving the city? Interestingly, I was now aware that I was not the only one that had started this meeting with a pre-conceived notion of the other person.

After the tour of the barber shop was completed, Mr. Butler said, "Show me the location of your project." Taking advantage of this shift in attitude, I cleared my calendar and brought Mr. Butler down to the 200 block of North Madeira Street.

By the end of the day, I had almost a half dozen "missed calls" from my friend.

Location, Location, Location

The single most important feature of a real estate project is location because it is permanent. I was confident that the properties on Madeira, albeit in deplorable and delapidated shape, were perfectly located to benefit from the growth of the Johns Hopkins Hospital. The challenge rested in building a superior, well priced product that would entice home ownership in a redevelopment neighborhood.

Although the 200 block of North Madeira Street was characterized by blight and vacancy, the street was a manageable redevelopment project because it was small. There were a total of 20 units on the street, and as of September of 2013, Tu Casa owned 6 of them. There were two homeowners and two renters that inhabited the street. Over time, Tu Casa would come to own 10 properties, or 50% of the total units on the block. This quiet, one-way street was now perfectly positioned for measurable redevelopment.

The original condition of the units on Madeira was nothing short of horrendous. According to the Baltimore City land records, the row homes were built in 1910. The sidewalk and street were in grave need of repair, but were always impeccably swept. I noticed that a resident kept them clean. The interiors of the structures were completely uninhabitable and had been vacant and exposed to the elements for decades. There were trees growing inside several of the units. Most of the vacant properties on the block were not properly boarded up and housed an infinite number of cats. They had also become a depository for trash and graffiti.

225 North Madeira and 221 North Madeira Original Interiors

The fronts of the buildings were in serious need of repair. Some units had formstone over the original brick fronts. Other units just had brick that had been painted or had deteriorated over the years.

221 North Madeira
Original Formstone Front

225 North Madeira
Original Old Brick Front

The backs of the properties were as challenging as the interiors. The backs were characterized by overgrown trees, much to my chagrin some of them growing inside the foundation of the homes. There was so much debris and filth that it was hard to imagine these structures could be successfully redeveloped.

221, 223, and 225 North Madeira Original Backs

Mr. Butler and I walked up and down the 200 block several times and then ventured into the alleys located behind the row homes. There was a drunk that had passed out behind one of the units, a white male that reeked of alcohol and too many body odors to list. I was disturbed and started to back up when Mr. Butler went straight to the individual, helped him up, and asked me if I had any bottled water in my car. After stumbling a bit to find his balance, the man walked away. Mr. Butler turned to me and said, "You should build parking pads behind the odd numbered homes. The alley is wide enough to fit a car." He never really acknowledged helping the man.

Mr. Butler continued to evaluate the location. He did not make eye contact with me and never removed his black Ray Bans. After approximately a half hour, he said, "I don't think I am interested". Surprised by the comment, I decided it was time to let Mr. Butler know that we had something substantial in common. I thought that telling him that I was a minority might precipitate a change of mind and said, "by the way, I am Puerto Rican". He stared at me and said, "Lady, that just makes it worse." We exchanged contact information and left Madeira.

Mr. Butler called a few days after our introductory meeting and said he would work with Tu Casa if he could build all 6 units. I immediately recognized that there was a very sharp business man behind those impenetrable Ray Bans. We came to an agreement on price, and executed a construction contract for the first unit with a verbal understanding that he would build the remaining 5 units. In retrospect, I realize that Mr. Butler trusted me first. We waited for the final settlement of the purchase of the houses from the City to begin construction. Years later, after Mr. Butler had become Kevin, I asked him why he decided to work me. He candidly responded, "Two reasons, I liked your vision and you also wore Ray Bans".

I now had a general contractor...Tu Casa Development Group LLC was ready to build on Madeira!

Trust

"The best way to find out if you can trust somebody is to trust them."
-Ernest Hemingway

Choosing the right contractor will be the second most important decision you will make, period. It is vital to identify a good general contractor. By good I mean excellent at the trade, easy to communicate with, and above all, trustworthy. I've seen solid projects fail and good intentioned individuals lose money due to contractor issues.

The general contractor's work will define you. This individual's final product will be an extension of you and it will positively or negatively impact your image as a developer. You want to find someone that is disciplined and driven, with a sense of pride and responsibility regarding their product. Above all, you must work with someone you can trust.

Additionally, a significant time of your day will likely include your contractor. You want to interact with someone that will be positive and driven. Recognize that real estate development can be a 24/7 venture and make a personal commitment to be available. "Life Happens" and there will be a constant source of issues, from site specific items, to city matters, to neighborhood dynamics, to an alarm going off at 3 o'clock in the morning. The possibilities are endless!

I knew that I would accomplish much more in a collaborative effort. I needed to be able to trust my general contractor. I found myself establishing my new company on an old concept, trust. However, the tricky thing about trust is that it has to be earned, and that takes time. Another complicating factor about trust is that it is not quantifiable because it is a sensation. I was just going to have to trust my gut feelings about Mr. Kevin Butler.

Over time I would come to realize that I had found a general contractor with all of these qualities, and many more.

Community Association

Caring Active Restoring Efforts (C.A.R.E.) is the community association that includes the 200 block of North Madeira Street. One of the reasons I was comfortable developing on Madeira was because of C.A.R.E. I attended a community association meeting to enlist support for the redevelopment effort and was exposed to the passion of the residents. I view passion as an invaluable and powerful intangible asset.

During the course of the meeting, it was clear that the leadership and residents of C.A.R.E. were united in their commitment to the Middle East neighborhood of Baltimore City. The arguments were quite heated and I was impressed by the passion in the discussions. Two hours into the meeting, I presented my redevelopment plans for the 200 block of North Madeira Street. I expected the community to welcome the efforts and thank me for targeting their neighborhood for redevelopment. Much to my chagrin, that would not happen, not at that meeting. My final message to those in attendance was that as much as I liked the location, I would not develop on the block without community support. In my final words, I promised to not to disappoint.

I received a letter of support from C.A.R.E. approximately one week after the meeting. I was thrilled! Drew Bennett, the C.A.R.E. President at the time, and Beth Myers-Edwards, Director of Community Engagements of Banner Neighborhoods Community Corporation, proved to be invaluable sources of information.

I was very excited to be developing in a neighborhood full of vibrant and passionate individuals.

Part Two:
"We Built"

Interior of 221 North Madeira, Before and After

Wreaths

The first step in fighting blight on the block was to properly board up all the vacant properties owned by Tu Casa. I decided to paint the "windows" white and the doors "Tu Casa Green." Mr. Butler thought that was a wonderful idea, and I paid him to buy the materials and complete the work. This relatively small investment helped fight blight significantly. The street looked quite clean and tidy. "Tu Casa Green" was the nickname for the sage green (Behr Dried Basil) paint used on all the Tu Casa property doors.

Neatly Boarded-up Vacant Properties

I decided to add a special pre-holiday touch, wreaths! I will never forget the day I told Mr. Butler that I wanted to hang holiday wreaths on the "windows" of the boarded up properties. I had a car full of wreaths and had spent all weekend making bows. He very calmly and pointedly said, "You want to do what?" I explained the whole concept of making the street look more festive and project health by decorating it with wreaths. The green wreaths with purple bows would look beautiful on the white painted windows. Purple was the color of the Tu Casa logo and The Baltimore Ravens, the city's beloved football team.

Mr. Butler looked at me and said, "Lady, I do not pay my men to hang wreaths. They are construction workers, not decorators." Greatly disappointed, I left the wreaths inside one of the units. After all, what was I going to do with 15 wreaths?

Two weeks later I came to Madeira and every wreath was perfectly positioned in the middle of each white "window."

Ready! Set! Go!

The day came when construction of the first unit was to begin. I was so excited! After more than 25 years living in the suburbs, it was time to explore the world of the inner city. I traded my Escalade for a fuel efficient car and my St. John's suits for blue jeans and hoodies. I substituted my designer flats with comfortable sneakers. Diana was ready to navigate incognito in Downtown Baltimore...or so I thought. My first day "on the job" everyone in the neighborhood was asking Mr. Butler who the blonde lady was. So much for going unnoticed!

The first unit developed was #212 and construction began in September of 2011. Located at the corner of Mullikin and Madeira Streets, the side of this unit framed the entrance to the 200 block. Mr. Butler suggested repointing the brick on the side of the unit as opposed to applying stucco as a finish. It was a wonderful suggestion. The perfectly repointed brick wall provided a nice, new focal entry point to the block and immediately projected health and revitalization.

I showed up on Madeira, camera in hand, ready to carefully photograph every step of the rehabilitation of the first unit. I had so many Kodak moments in mind! I was wearing some very comfortable flats, blue jeans and a Boys' Latin School of Maryland (BL) sweatshirt. BL is a magnificent college preparatory school that my husband and I entrusted with educating two of our children.

My joy was short-lived. As soon as he saw me, the contractor said, "Lady, stay off my construction site with those ballerina slippers. You are going to end up with a nail in your foot!" No "Good Morning Mrs. Gaines," no smile, just a very stern look. Ballerina slippers? I was wearing carefully chosen flat shoes! For once in my life, I was speechless. For those that know me, I am a lot of things, and one of them is not speechless. That curt voice then added, "Next time you want to visit the construction site, you ask for my permission. Lady, you are bad for business."

My first reaction was anger. One thing about Hispanic women, don't make us angry. Who did this man think he was talking to? After all, it was my construction site, not his. I was the "Lady" with the money! I was the boss! (The term "Boss Lady" was coined shortly thereafter. Once it even popped up as graffiti on the cement of a newly poured sidewalk square). I kept my thoughts to myself and made a mental note to work on Mr. Butler's attitude. I seriously doubted my choice of general contractor. This venture was going to be a lot of things, and fun seemed not to be one of them.

I am a very talkative individual by nature. Much to my chagrin, I discovered that, other than when he was "unhappy" with me, Mr. Butler was a man of few words. He could answer the majority of my questions with one of three words: "No", "Yes" and "OK". Over time, Mr. Butler's vocabulary did expand to include one sentence, "I'll call you later," and body language. "I'll call you later" meant the answer was "no" but he wanted to wait to say it. The worst response resulted when he walked away mid-sentence. That was the Butler equivalent of saying "talk to the hand."

I did not let Mr. Butler's demeanor deter me and took many photos of Step One, the demolition process. In hind sight, I do believe I stayed on Madeira longer than I needed to just to assert my position as the developer of the project. It was certainly an unspoken battle of the wills between developer and contractor. Confident that I had obtained all the photos necessary to adequately illustrate the demolition process, I said my good-bye's to whoever would listen and left the site. I was later further reprimanded by Mr. Butler and told not to ever speak to the workers again.

Approximately ten minutes after leaving Madeira my cell phone rang and a voice said, "What is your shoe size?" The rest of the conversation went as follows:

Diana- "Who is this?"
Kevin- "It's Kevin"
Diana- "Kevin?"
Kevin- "Yes, Kevin Butler, the contractor on Madeira."
Awkward Silence...
Diana- "What?"
Kevin- "What is your shoe size?"
Diana- "I am a size 9, why?"
Kevin- "OK. If you are going to visit the construction site I am going to have to buy you a pair of construction boots."

And so my relationship with Mr. Kevin Butler began to define itself. *I instantly recognized that underneath that distant demeanor there was a remarkable individual.*

Demolition and Gutting

Mr. Butler taught me that the only way to be able to fully control quality and avoid unwanted surprises in the finished product was to decrease the variables during the rehabilitation process. In vacant property construction, it meant eliminating them by completely demolishing the interior of a unit. Thus, our approach to preparing a unit for construction on Madeira was uniform and simple. Step One was and always is to gut the unit down to the foundation and the firewalls. A concrete slab was then poured on the ground of the gutted unit. Rebuilding the dwelling required all new materials and translated into higher construction costs, but profit was secondary to the redevelopment effort.

225 Complete Gut of Unit

Demolition provided the opportunity to discover hidden treasures. Mr. Butler called my searches through the rubble "Diana's field trips." I discovered a clay marble that was manufactured in Germany in 1898 and many apothecary bottles dating back to the early 1900's. These items were a reminder of the history and the age of the homes we were redeveloping.

In the beginning, Mr. Butler was simply appalled that I would rummage through rubble in search of items. I did pick up several items that were not collectibles, and Mr. Butler was very quick to help me identify those. One of my favorite "field trip moments" occurred in the winter of 2013, when Kevin and I were evaluating a very large site for potential redevelopment. The original condition of this location was truly frightening. Most of the dwellings had no backs and many party walls were simply missing. As we were walking around the properties I noticed that Kevin picked up a glass bottle. He never said a word, and just handed it to me. I tried not to smile.

The approach of gutting down to the foundation and the firewalls did differentiate Tu Casa's product. The interesting thing is that as potential homebuyers, we all make decisions based on what we can see: trey ceilings, granite countertops, gleaming hardwood floors. *However, when it comes to the rehabilitation of a property, what lies behind the dry wall is much more important than what lies in front of it.*

Brick Repointing

The units on the 200 block of North Madeira had formstone or badly damaged brick exteriors. Formstone, a cement-based, simulated stone material, was very popular as an exterior application to the fronts of Baltimore row homes beginning in the late 1930's. The less affluent neighborhoods of early Baltimore had homes made with porous and brittle bricks. The narrower, two-bay wide rowhomes located on Madeira were definitely part of that inventory. Formstone was an affordable alternative applied to the brick fronts that created a seal and blocked leaks.

Brick repointing is the process of restoring brick to its original condition. It is a very interesting and involved process that requires knowledge and craftsmanship.

Original Brick

Prepped Brick

Repointed Brick

The underlaying brick is washed down and treated before any mortar is repaired. The external part of the mortar joints is cut out and removed either by hand using a small chisel or with a power masonry blade. The mortar is cut to a depth that slightly exceeds the width of the joint, carefully digging out the horizontal joints first, then the vertical ones.

New mortar is made to match the color of the original mortar and is set with a trowel at the level of the face of the brick.

Repairing Mortar

In the final step, the wall is brushed and the recently repointed brick looks brand new.

Every home developed by Tu Casa on the street has a repointed brick front. *One by one, Earl and his workers restored the brick fronts of every Tu Casa unit on the 200 block of North Madeira Street.*

Basement Digging and Underpinning

Most Baltimore City row homes are characterized by having unfinished basements with crawl space. In an effort to differentiate the row homes on Madeira and attract homebuyers using a value added approach, Tu Casa offered completely finished basements with 7+ foot ceilings and ceramic tile floors. We even included surround sound systems in the earlier units. This was a virtually unoccupied street, and Tu Casa had to make the homes attractive through features and value to encourage home purchasing.

224 North Madeira Basement Dug by Hand

In order to achieve the ceiling height, the basements were dug by hand, often taking almost 6 weeks to complete. Digging a deeper basement also meant doing significant underpinning to maintain the structural integrity of the dwelling. Proper basement underpinning is a paramount component of the rehabilitation process. *I made sure to carefully document every step of the process through photographs that were shared with potential buyers.*

Framing and Systems

Framing is one of my favorite parts of the rehabilitation process, as it is the first indication that the dwelling will be a home. Wood frame construction is the leading method of building homes in the United States. Lumber is the most popular construction framing material because it is strong, durable, readily available, and easy to work with. Materials such as steel, brick and concrete that can support more weight than wood may also be used to frame.

Butler Management did platform-frame construction. First floor joists were completely covered with sub-flooring, effectively forming a platform on which exterior walls and interior partitions were raised. Once the framing was completed, the electrical, HVAC and plumbing systems were installed.

The location of the windows and the width of the unit drove the determination to build a split-foyer or traditional floor plan. The split foyer floor plans were Mr. Butler's idea and they proved to be popular and attractive. They maximized the amount of light that entered the unit, especially in the finished basement. It is during framing that you can make any necessary adjustments to the floor plan, and we often did. Mr. Butler and I would walk the property and discuss specifics. The use of L-shape or vertical stairwells varied depending on the width and the depth of the unit. Our goal was simple, to maximize living space.

Once the framing was completed the layout was analyzed for fluency and size. Outlets, vent locations and cable TV connections were identified. I remember the first time I saw an electrical outlet perfectly centered in the wall of the living area. All I could think of was how absolutely "wrong" that outlet looked. It reminded me of a townhouse that Steve and I purchased and the builder had placed electrical outlets in the ceilings.

My conversation with Mr. Butler, who I had started to address as Kevin approximately four months into the construction process, went as follows. Please know that when I ask "What is that?" I am really saying "I don't like that." Also, when Kevin does not respond it means he is annoyed.

Diana- "What is that?"
Kevin- Pause. No initial response. "It's an electrical outlet".
Diana- "I know what it is. Why is it there?"
Kevin- "Why not?"
Diana- "It's a weird location."
Kevin- "No it's not. Homebuyers want TV's in their living areas. It is much more cost efficient to put an outlet in now than have the buyers pay an electrician after they move in."
Diana- Silence
Kevin- "Do you want me to remove it?"
Diana- "No".
Kevin- Big smile

Kevin and I had countless exchanges like that over the course of the redevelopment of a unit. He was very patient and took the time to answer all of my why and what questions in great detail. I became so knowledgeable about construction! I also learned to never question Mr. Butler when it came to materials, placement of outlets, and just about anything that had to do with the construction of the house. Truth is, he was always right.

About those electrical outlets placed on the walls, most of the buyers did place flat screen televisions in the living area and the ones that didn't covered the outlets with art.

Drywall

Once all of the systems were in satisfactory condition and the necessary inspections were completed, it was time to install the drywall. Drywall, (also known as plasterboard, wallboard, gypsum board, sheetrock, or gyprock), is the material used to make interior walls and ceilings. The drywall added a feeling of permanence to the home. Once the drywall was completed, walls were painted and light fixtures, vent covers, doors and all other interior finishes were incorporated into the house.

It was primarily during the framing and drywall phases that Mr. Butler and I truly learned to work together. He focused on construction and I focused on refining the design. We often problem solved collectively and the end result was a better product. Pleased with the results of the business collaboration, our conversations started to shift from purely business discussions to childhood experiences, family, and philosophy. I found out that Kevin does not believe in luck. He used to say, "There is no such thing as luck. It is hard work and discipline that create opportunity." I also discovered that Mr. Butler was a natural entrepreneur with a remarkable affinity for finance. We started discussing the pro's and con's of investing in the stock market vs. precious metal futures.

I made an effort to wear boots during construction site visits and Kevin stopped wearing the Ray Bans. I also started to notice that Kevin seemed to know "everyone" in the city. Between friends from the neighborhood, friends from school, and acquaintances from his years doing construction, Kevin Butler certainly knew a wide range of Baltimoreans.

Development was occurring at a steady pace. Tu Casa' s houses were one step closer to becoming someone' s home, and Mrs. Gaines and Mr. Butler were on their way to establishing a friendship.

Interior Finishes

Tu Casa's goal was to establish itself as one of Baltimore City's developers of choice, bridging the gap between the need for quality redevelopment and a demand for luxury, affordable homes. Thus, the interior finishes of Tu Casa's homes consisted of high quality materials like hardwood floors and granite counter tops. The goal with the interiors was to create a perfectly appointed house that a buyer could convert into their home with a small additional investment in window treatments. The entrances featured gleaming hardwood floors and 9 foot ceilings. A powder room was placed off the hallways that lead to the kitchens.

225 Main Floor Living Area

The modern kitchens featured hardwood floors, granite countertops, wood cabinets and new, stainless steel appliances.

Modern Kitchens

The second levels included two bedrooms and two full bathrooms, a laundry area with stackable washer and dryer, and access to a fenced-in patio or roof top deck. The bathrooms included elaborate tile work and jet tubs.

Elaborate Tile Work, Jet Tub

The basements were fully finished, with ceramic tile floors and 7+ foot ceilings. They were clean and spacious and were often described by potential purchasers as the perfect family rooms.

221 North Madeira Finished Basement

In order to maintain the integrity of the market value of the homes, the quality of the materials was consistent among the units developed.

Patterns and colors were altered to ensure that each home had its own personality.

Exterior Finishes

As Mr. Butler had noted during his first visit to Madeira, the odd numbered units backed to an alley that was wide enough to fit a vehicle. This afforded Tu Casa the opportunity to offer cement parking pads located in the rear of these units. Being able to provide private parking pads proved to be a remarkable marketing advantage for "Casitas at Madeira".

The backs of the units were finished with stucco. Stucco is a popular exterior finish for row homes because it is fire, rust and rot resistant. Stucco can also be tinted and finished in a wide range of colors and textures.

Finished Backs of 221, 223 and 225 North Madeira
Private Cement Parking Pads

The inclusion of wood decks added an attractive outdoor living feature to the units on Madeira. New homeowners were able to place patio furniture and flower pots on their decks. We also built fenced in areas for privacy.

In the spring of 2013, Kevin purchased two vacant properties on Mullikin Street that were slated for demolition. He built a roof top deck on one of the units and it was fantastic. I will never forget the view from the deck. It added another completely new dimension to city living. Roof top decks became a standard feature on all future units developed by Tu Casa and asking prices were increased by $10,000. The decks were incredibly well received.

In an effort to increase illumination and safety on the street, all Tu Casa homes had dual entrance lighting and a camera-based, intercom system. The intercom system was Kevin's idea. Tu Casa homeowners could see an image of who was knocking on their doors through these handy devices.

A gardening fanatic, I included brick flower boxes on the front of every unit. A gentleman called Rob built all of the brick steps and flower boxes. He rode his bicycle to Madeira. Rob was very skilled and had an excellent disposition. The flower boxes were my favorite exterior feature of the units. *The growing number of planted flower boxes were firm symbols that revitalization was taking place on the 200 block of North Madeira Street.*

Reasonable Risk

When I first started developing on Madeira, I was extremely cautious about where I parked, where I walked, and what I did. Frankly, I was a bit afraid of the City. Mr. Butler would accompany me if I left Madeira. He often walked me to the car. My comfort level steadily increased the more I visited the project and I started to walk alone. I discovered that the key to safety was basic, using common sense. I now walk with confidence in the footprint of the C.A.R.E. neighborhood. One day, Kevin and I walked three blocks to the 200 block of Duncan Street through alleys and back streets. Kevin said, "Imagine that, Diana Gaines walking through alleys in Baltimore City." It was the first time I realized that I had become completely comfortable navigating the city by foot.

It was important to add some elements to the redevelopment effort that generated future resident confidence and promoted increased safety on Madeira. My goal was to create an environment where it was acceptable to take a risk. Features like the camera based intercom system and alarm systems were incorporated as standard in Tu Casa's product. Dual entrance lighting was also important. Two bulbs provided greater illumination along the perimeter of the street as compared to a single light fixture. The street became increasingly well-lit as the homes were redeveloped, sold and subsequently occupied.

The only time I ever felt in danger on Madeira occurred about 2 weeks before #212 was to go to settlement. I opened the door and attempted to deactivate the alarm system. To my surprise, the system was off. I turned around and saw an empty wine bottle on the floor. My immediate response was anger. I called Kevin and was literally screaming at the top of my lungs, completely offended that someone had a "party" on my property.

I am not proud of the language I used to express my dissatisfaction. However, the angry screams likely saved me. As I walked up the steps and looked in the bathroom I started to shake. There was a pair of blue jeans, socks, shoes, a toothbrush and a cell phone on the counter! I was certain that I was going to be the headline of the five o'clock news that evening. I have never been more in fear for my life. I ran down the steps, left the unit and called the police. I still remember the fear I felt, especially as I turned my back to run.

A police inspection revealed that a 40" Flat Screen TV located in the basement had been stolen. (A television had been installed in the basement as a special gift for the project's first buyer). The perpetrator had obviously spent the night in the house, removed the TV at nightfall, and had been sleeping upstairs when I entered the house. The offender had likely escaped through the upstairs deck. There was so much evidence left behind that I was sure the thief would be identified. After all, a cell phone had been left at the scene. I inquired several times about the status of the case and eventually gave up. Baltimore City had greater crimes to solve.

The morning after the break-in, a new TV had been installed and any damage to the walls had been fully repaired. Kevin indicated that he was at fault for not setting the alarm the night before.

Mr. Butler had taken full responsibility for the incident, repaired the damage, and replaced the flat screen TV.

Part Three:
"They Came"

Back of Odd-Numbered Units, Before and After

The Market Talks...Listen!

It is very important to continuously gauge market demand. It is even more important to recognize what the market wants and adjust your strategy and product offerings accordingly. At one point, there were two finished units on the market, #221 and #222. I began to hear comments like "I prefer the color of the floor in #222 but I like the granite in #221." This prompted the idea of offering a pre-development purchase option. Until now, all units sold had been purchased "as is", with no input from the buyer. The pre-development purchase option was named the "C3" Program, which stood for Tu Casa's Custom Choices. In exchange for a binding contract, Tu Casa agreed to let the homebuyer select interior finishes from a grouping of materials that the general contractor would provide. The only obstacle between "C3" and implementation was my general contractor. Now I had to convince Mr. Butler that this was a good idea.

The first time I approached Kevin about the mini-custom option he was not pleased. Kevin looked at me and said, "Can't do it. Now we are building customs on Madeira?" By this point I had been working with Mr. Butler long enough to know that his first response to anything I asked was generally "no". He would then take the time to analyze the added value of the effort and randomly, often late at night, text the word "OK" to my cell phone. I debated that there was no difference between Diana Gaines approving interior finish materials or someone else choosing from selections that he provided. I further established to have the buyers select the materials within 30 days of contract ratification. I argued that with this procedure in place the construction timeline would not be delayed, (Kevin's primary concern), by buyer decisions. Approximately one week after the Custom Choices discussion, I received a text at 10:00pm one evening, "OK". Tu Casa' s "C3" Program was official!

Tu Casa's "C3" Program allowed the buyer to choose design details that expressed their personal preferences. With Kevin's help, I prepared tablets called "Tu Choice" Selection Tablets. Options included hardwood floor, interior paint color, kitchen counter granite, kitchen cabinets, and floor and accent ceramic tile for the bathrooms. Mr. Butler was very generous with selections and buyers often had over a dozen samples of granite and tile to choose from. A "mini-custom" home was now available on Madeira for the price of a non-custom home.

Tu Casa received 2 pre-construction contracts in 36 hours!

The Block Captain

When we began construction on Madeira, there were 2 existing homeowners, two rental properties, and three dozen cats. There was a young man, Rob, who represented a third generation on Madeira. Like his grandfather and father before him, Rob had always lived on the 200 block of North Madeira Street. Rob's family owned two homes that were located next to each other. Rob welcomed the redevelopment of the street with a very positive attitude. He was a zealous and intense Raven's fan, and many potential buyers experienced Rob's fan fest. Rob kept me informed of any occurrences on Madeira. No incident was too insignificant to report to Diana. I welcomed these phone calls and made sure to address any issues or concerns.

Rob was the resident that kept the street clean on a daily basis. Approximately 18 months into the redevelopment efforts on Madeira, the city of Baltimore rebuilt the sidewalks and resurfaced the street. The results were outstanding! The 200 Block of North Madeira Street became an example of community cooperation at its finest: a developer rehabilitating the units, the city improving the surrounding infrastructure, and a resident maintaining it all clean and tidy.

Rob was designated as the Block Captain and I can honestly say that the 200 of North Madeira Street was a cleaner and safer place when Rob was home. As the transformation of the 200 block of North Madeira progressed, it became very evident that it was important to identify resources to help Rob with the rehabilitation of his home. Millions of dollars were being allocated to demolition in Baltimore City, and it was imperative that some dollars be allocated to assist existing homeowners, like Rob, that were caught in the middle of a redevelopment area.

There were two lovely women that rented on Madeira when we started construction, Ms. Lois and Ms. Bernice. They were always kind and friendly. Ms. Bernice invited me into her home one day. It was beautiful! It was the first time I had seen exposed brick in the interior of a home. Tu Casa began to offer interior brick repointing as an option. Ms. Lois was a minister. I did her a small favor and she told me her congregation was praying for me. Prayers are a divine gift; I felt so blessed!

In the fall of 2013, Rob called and asked to meet in person and told me his family had lost one of the houses. He wanted me to buy it and added that his grandfather would of wanted me to revitalize the home.

This was a uniquely humbling experience. This man had just lost his house and he wanted me to buy it for redevelopment. I can honestly say that this was one of the highlights of my journey on Madeira.

Rob' s words were a confirmation that Tu Casa had reached its community objective of being recognized as a trustworthy and reliable developer.

Demolition for New Sidewalks

Cats

The story of the 200 block of North Madeira Street would not be complete if I failed to write about the feline population that inhabited the street when we started development. Madeira's vacant structures were home to about 3 dozen cats, and the street, surrounding alleys and empty lots were their litter box. The cats were wild and nasty and multiplying at an alarming rate. Calls to Animal Control were fruitless, the answer always the same: "too many cats and nowhere to put them." The only positive was that the cats kept the rats to minimal numbers. The first time I saw a city rat I thought it was an opossum!

Kevin Butler was amused by my efforts to rescue cats. He helped me set up safe traps and monitored them. I made him promise that if he ever found kittens inside a Tu Casa home he would call. He simply responded, "I can do that." The cat population did steadily decrease as we developed more homes.

The first rescue was a female kitten with grey stripes. As soon as I brought her home the kids started to call her Mia. Well, Mia in Spanish means mine. She became a Gaines. Two years later I am pleased to say that Mia is alive and well, all 12 pounds of her!

In October of 2011, my cell phone rang and it was Kevin.

Kevin- "I have one"
Diana – "You have one what"
Kevin- "A kitten"
Diana- "A what?"
Kevin- "You said to call you if I found a kitten. We found one doing the demo for #225. It is at Rob's house in a shoebox."

The kids and I drove to Madeira and found a tiny little creature, eyes shut, resembling a rodent more than a cat. We named the kitten "Maddie", for Madeira, and rushed it to the vet. After a careful examination, "Maddie" became "Mattie". The vet said the kitten was about a week old. We all fed Mattie by hand, every two hours, for 4 weeks. As time passed, Mattie started to gain weight, opened his eyes, and would knead and purr when held. One morning, during a 3:00am feeding, Mattie had a seizure, and I took it to a 24 hour Animal Hospital. The kitten was in an incubator, fed intravenously, and every effort was made to save it. Five days later, Mattie died. The kitten had been born with a congenital disease, and that is why it had been abandoned inside the old house.

"New Baltimoreans" on Madeira

The "New Baltimoreans" that live on the 200 Block of North Madeira Street are all extraordinary individuals. They identified a great opportunity to purchase a well built, comfortable and affordable home in a neighborhood that was transitioning. They shared the opinion that their homes would appreciate within a reasonable timeframe. They came together to form a community, and it was wonderful to watch.

Tu Casa and Butler Management rebuilt the bricks and mortar on the 200 block of Madeira Street, but the new homeowners gave it new life. Every home buyer on Madeira was part of something greater than their individual home purchases, the revitalization of an entire Baltimore City block.

The first buyer was Ryan. He was an excellent anchor for the 200 block of North Madeira Street. He was relocating from Georgia to Maryland with the Army and wanted to live in the city. Ryan's unit was the only one developed at the time of acquisition. A second unit, #221, was under construction. This young man and his realtor had great faith in this woman developer. About the realtor, her name was Kim Jones, and she was amazing! She used to call me "Lady Diana" and she was truly delightful to work with. A woman of incredible faith, Kim loved her family, her job and her God.

The buyers that followed Ryan were a pleasure to work with. Many of the residents worked with a fantastic Home Mortgage Consultant by the name of Sean Worrall. Sean proved to be very skillful and helpful in combining mortgage financing and homebuyer incentives. I referred many propective buyers to Sean due to his knowledge, hard work, dedication, and availability.

Marjorie visited Madeira a half dozen times before buying. Approximately a week after settlement she sent a short but lovely email, "I love my home." The first time I met Daria, I opened the door, she stepped in and said, "I want it. I want to buy this house." After settlement, she had the majority of the rooms painted with vibrant colors.

Matt bought his home half way through the construction process and was the first buyer to take advantage of the Custom Choices Program. He did an excellent job combining colors and materials. James and Amanda and later Stephanie, purchased houses before the Building

Permits were issued! They truly took advantage of the "C3" Program. They were able to provide significant input into the design and lay-out of their homes.

Andrea and Steve, newlyweds, had been house hunting for over a year. They did a fabulous job incorporating personal touches to their home. Jason was the ultimate entrepreneur. The first time I met him he was holding two dozen index cards, each representing a different address in his home search. Madeira was stop number four and I sincerely hoped he would come back and buy a unit. He did!

Jason

The 200 block of North Madeira Street was alive, and the growing number of individual property lights that illuminated the block at night were the evidence.

Madeira Recognized

Kevin had always advised me to maintain a low profile. He was a firm believer in minding your own business, no exceptions. I followed his advice for the first year and a half of development. However, the more we built and the more properties that were sold, the more attention the block drew. It became increasingly difficult to maintain anonymity.

Monyka Berrocosa, Founder of MyCity4HER, an entrepreneurial advocate and champion of women in business, wrote the first article about the redevelopment effort on Madeira. "M", as friends call her, was very kind to me and became a steady source of confidence and inspiration. Other journalists wrote subsequent articles, including Pedro Palomino of **SomosBaltimoreLatino.com**, an online magazine for the Latino community. Pedro is a true blessing of a reporter to the Hispanic community.

The 200 Block of North Madeira became an example of the Vacants to Value Program's success and Baltimore Housing showcased the project often. Visitors included Mayor Rawlings-Blake, the Cable News Network (CNN), State and city representatives, and numerous out of town delegations. Tu Casa was featured in a developer video on the V2V Program website and was described as reliable and committed.

In July of 2013, the Mayor's Office organized a Task Force called the "New Americans Task Force" and I was invited to be part of the effort. I was assigned as a Co-Chair of the Housing Committee. I recommended changing the name of the task force to "New Baltimoreans" and the recommendation was adopted. Working on the task force afforded me the opportunity to expand my knowledge base regarding the city and its dynamics. I was also introduced to some remarkable leaders, all unified by the vision of a better Baltimore.

The Task Force opened my eyes to the growing number of immigrants calling Baltimore City home on a daily basis. I tried very hard to develop a program that could accommodate the immigrant community. I wanted the dream of homeownership to be available to all Baltimoreans. Unfortunately, credit was not readily available to this new group of Baltimoreans, and I was not able to complete a sale to a member of the growing immigrant community.

The rewards and accolades originated by the redevelopment efforts on Madeira started to become somewhat overwhelming. In 2013, the Baltimore Sun identified yours truly as one of the "50 Women to Watch" in Baltimore and The Maryland Hispanic Chamber of Commerce (MDHCC) named Tu Casa Development Group the 2013 Outstanding Small Business of the Year. Veronica Namnun Cool, a remarkable business woman, handed me the MDHCC award. I was humbled to be recognized by fellow Hispanic businessmen and women and to be chosen from such an accomplished slate of nominees. In April of 2014, Smart CEO Magazine presented a Brava! Award and in May of 2014, I received a Trailblazer Award from the Center Club's Women in Business Intraclub.

I had started this journey with the goal of personal growth, not public recognition. When I was younger, I spent many, many years working 80+ hour weeks. I was aggressive, driven and unstoppable in my quest to succeed. I never made a social difference all those years. Now, at age 50, I had reinvented myself in a venture that positively impacted many lives. It felt fundamentally good to be able to permanently and positively improve the city's landscape and to be recognized for inspiring other women in business.

After my family, the 200 block of North Madeira Street felt like my greatest accomplishment.

Mentorship

In August of 2013, I received a Custom Form Submission through the Tu Casa website from a young man named Michael Henley. The message read as follows: "Dear Mrs. Gaines: My name is Michael Henley. I read about you in the Baltimore Sun and several websites. I am writing you because I have been searching for a mentor. I want to learn about real estate development."

I felt very conflicted when I received this request. I was very busy at the time. Kevin Butler was the construction expert, and I was quite sure he would not agree to a mentorship. Kevin already had an apprentice, and her name was Diana. However, I firmly believe in "paying it forward". I had gained a significant amount of knowledge regarding construction and was open to sharing it. I decided to learn more about this young man and asked him to provide some background information and prepare a paragraph addressing why he wanted to learn about real estate development.

Michael's answers touched my heart. He started his response by stating that his mother taught him at a very young age that he could learn more by listening than talking, and that he therefore found it very hard to write about himself. What great wisdom this young man expressed! He said he considered accomplishments to be blessings that were reached with the help of others and described himself as a Christian and a family man.

Michael added that he wanted to learn real estate development because when he was young, his mother purchased a boarded up home in what he described as "a better neighborhood". Once the house was fully renovated, Michael and his sister got the opportunity to move to a nicer area and attend better schools. He indicated that he could identify with Tu Casa's mission because he understood how real estate could impact someone's life, as he was a product of it. He felt that the renovation of the vacant home was the catalyst that led to more opportunities in his life. He ended his correspondence by stating that "It is my goal to one day go back and redevelop my old neighborhood."

Of course I mentored Michael, and I really enjoyed sharing my knowledge and experiences with such a fine young man. Over the course of approximately 6 months, Michael visited Madeira several times and was able to see the different stages of development of the Tu Casa row homes. I also shared a wealth of written information with him during that period. I prepared some manuals that documented the rehabilitation process with words and photographs.

Michael and I continue to exchange information. I firmly believe that he will achieve his real estate redevelopment goals. *It was a sincere pleasure to share part of my journey with him.*

Final Thoughts

I encourage everyone reading these pages to find their personal completion to the question "Why not?" You never know what professional and personal growth that simple yet potentially complicated query could lead to. As you identify and understand the nature of your "Why not?" your life will be permanently transformed. For Diana Torruella Gaines, the growth was immeasurable, and this manuscript clearly identifies how.

As of July 31, 2014, Tu Casa's redevelopment efforts on the 200 block of North Madeira Street will have been completed and this venture will officially come to an end. Over the course of two years, Tu Casa's houses on Madeira became home to 12 "New Baltimoreans." They are all remarkable visionaries that played a critical role in making an ordinary street extraordinary. They converted Tu Casa's houses into their homes and truly gave life to the term "From Vacants to Value". Furthermore, I look forward to watching many firsts unfold on Madeira over the next decade: the first engagement, the first marriage, and the first baby!

He never said it, but I could tell that Mr. Kevin Butler was very proud to have played a pivotal role in redeveloping a part of Baltimore City, his City. I asked him if he ever showed his children what he had accomplished on Madeira. The best recognition he could ever receive came in the words of his 6 year old daughter, who upon visiting Madeira said, "Daddy, you did all of them?"

As homeownership increased, the 200 block of North Madeira Street steadily transformed from "House to Home", "Ordinary to Extraordinary" and "Vacants to Value", and this developer's journey in the Middle East neighborhood of Baltimore City came to an end. *What started out as an ordinary journey proved to be supremely extraordinary.*

Epilogue

The personal and professional growth experienced as a result of reinventing myself as a real estate developer was immeasurable. I truly hope to identify a new cluster of homes in the need of rehabilitation. I wish to "turn the lights on" in another Baltimore City block.

Mr. Kevin Butler has agreed to continue to work with Tu Casa, and this is very energizing. He indicated a need to retire by the age of 40, so I guess we have "four more years."

Rob's home on Madeira has yet to be improved. I sincerely hope to secure the necessary funds ($15,000) to refurbish the front of his house and make some minor interior modifications. He truly deserves it.

Three years after I started my original journey into the field of real estate development, I conclude my efforts exactly how I began... with my husband Steve as my banker and Mr. Kevin Butler as my general contractor, only this time in search of the "next Madeira."

Resources

http://www.mdfirsttimehomebuyer.com/index.shtml
http://www.boltonhill.org/mria/documents/chap/taxcredits/tc2.htm
http://www.baltimorehousing.org/
http://www.vacantstovalue.org/
http://www.baltimorehousing.org/property_registration
http://www.tax-rates.org/maryland/property-tax

About the Author

Diana T. Gaines was born and raised in Puerto Rico, where she attended Academia San José. She came to Baltimore in 1985, after graduating from Duke University. After a career in commercial lending specializing in healthcare followed by 12 years raising her three sons, she reinvented herself in 2010 as a real estate developer targeting rehabilitation properties. Redeveloping the 200 block of North Madeira Street in Baltimore, Maryland, became her new passion. The first Hispanic woman developer in the City, her goal is to provide "affordable luxury living options" to Baltimore City home buyers.

*In her free time, Diana loves to watch her children play baseball and go back to her native Puerto Rico to fish with her brother, Capt. Juan Carlos Torruella, aboard The Extremist, **www.extremefishingpuertorico.com**.*

"Awakening." – Kevin Butler, General Contractor

"When I first met Diana and Kevin in the summer of 2013, they shared their plan with me to repave the street, give us new sidewalks, put in parking and continue renovation of the vacant homes on the street. They have delivered and hit their mark. It's fun to see what positive change Tu Casa Development Group has brought to the 200 block of North Madeira" – Jason Allen, Homebuyer

"I'm currently under contract on a Tu Casa Development Group home on the 200 block of North Madeira Street. My boyfriend already owned one of Diana's homes and I wanted my first home to be built with the same quality and great features as his. Because I entered my contract pre-rehabilitation, I was given the freedom of picking my interior finishes. Working with Diana and Kevin has been great. I can't wait to settle!" – Stephanie Norton, Homebuyer

"Hacer realidad el sueño Americano es algo que Diana viene realizando con su projecto de "Casitas en Madeira". Es una hada madrina de los inmigrantes de Baltimore." Translation: "To make the American dream a reality is something that Diana has been accomplishing through her project "Casitas at Madeira". She is a fairy godmother to immigrants in Baltimore." – Pedro Palomino, Director, Somos Baltimore Latino

"I searched for a mentor that would be willing to teach me about their success and be humble enough to help me learn from their mistakes. Mrs. Gaines embodies this balance. It's truly a blessing to receive mentorship from her." – Michael Henley, Mentorship Recipient

"When my wife, Amanda, and I met Diana, it was immediately clear that she cared about the neighborhood she was helping to rebuild — probably even more than she cared about profit margins. That made it an easy decision to work with her." – James Briggs, Homebuyer

"By wisely leveraging the existing Vacants to Value Program from Baltimore City and her own financial investments, Diana transformed a section of Baltimore; making it a wonderfully welcoming place where friends and families thrive to grow into a neighborhood. "
- Veronica Namnun Cool,
Former Chairman, Maryland Hispanic Chamber of Commerce